Copyright ©2020 ARNOLD KUNTZ PH.D

CONTENTS

INTRODUCTION

If you're looking for a way to produce food while working with nature instead of against it, permaculture is your answer.

What is permaculture farming? Permaculture gives farmers a way to achieve high yields and productivity while doing it in a more sustainable and environmentally-friendly way than conventional farming methods. It applies a more holistic approach to farming crops or livestock.

In this article, you'll learn what permaculture is, the 12 principles of permaculture, its benefits, and several real-world permaculture practices.

WHAT IS PERMACULTURE?

Permaculture is an approach to agricultural design that focuses on whole systems thinking, as well as using or simulating patterns from nature.

The term originated from David Holmgren in 1978, but the practices of permaculture date back much further.

Permaculture has 3 core tenants:
1. Care for the earth. In other words, help all life systems continue to exist and multiply. Because if we don't have a healthy planet, humans can't exist at all.

2. Care for the people. Allow people to access resources they need to survive.

3. Fair share. You should only take what you need, and reinvest any surplus. Any extra can go forward to helping fulfill the two other core tenants. This includes returning waste products back into the system so it can be made useful again.

Conventional agriculture tends to work against nature, instead of with it.

We tear up whatever natural ecosystem was on the land before, and turn it into a blank slate that we can plant crops or raise livestock on. But there's another way.

By using principles of permaculture, you're working with nature, instead of against it. That means that you can let nature do most of the work for you.

THE 12 PRINCIPLES OF PERMACULTURE

David Holmgren's original ideas regarding permaculture can be broken down into twelve design principles.

1. Observe and Interact

Take time to observe nature before making any decisions or changes. Often just by observing, we can get a lot of insight into how to design our farm or garden to suit what's already there.

2. Catch and Store Energy

In nature, resources tend to come in peak periods. We get a lot of sunlight in the summer, but much less in the winter. In some places there are rainy seasons some of the time, and droughts other parts of the time.

Permaculture is big on capturing resources like rainwater or solar electricity so they can be used later as needed.

3. Obtain a Yield

Make sure you're being rewarded for the work that you're putting in. After all, you probably aren't farming just for a hobby. You want to get food, an income, or something else in return. You can't work on an empty stomach.

4. Apply Self-regulation and Accept Feedback

Hold yourself accountable, and also be open to suggestions and critiques from others. If there is something you're doing that's inappropriate for your situation, you want to know about it, so your systems can function well.

5. Use and Value Renewable Resources and Services

Nature has an abundance of renewable resources that we can make use of. We should prioritize those, and try to reduce the consumption of non-renewable resources.

6. Produce No Waste

Being "zero waste" is a big trend right now, but really it all started with permaculture. If we value all of the resources that we have available and use a bit of ingenuity, we can make sure that nothing goes to waste.

7. Design from Patterns to Details

Take a look at nature and society. You can usually observe patterns in things like how beehives are organized, the design on a snail shell, or other things to give inspiration for your designs.

You can borrow from these designs and add some details and flair of your own.

8. Integrate Rather Than Segregate

Permaculture is all about having things support each other and work together, instead of having everything exist as an island unto itself.

By pairing different plants, livestock, and other objects together correctly, we can take advantage of relationships they can have with each other.

9. Use Small and Slow Solutions

Permaculture isn't about making big changes overnight. Making gradual changes and working with slow systems makes them much easier to maintain.

Plus they tend to have a more sustainable outcome. When it comes to permaculture, slow and steady wins the race.

10. Use and Value Diversity

Where conventional farming is all about monoculture and many farmers traditionally only grow one or two crops, permaculture is big on diversity.

A diverse system is much less vulnerable to threats like pests, diseases, and other problems than a homogeneous one. Don't put your eggs all in one basket.

11. Use Edges and Value the Marginal

Where two different things meet is usually where the most interesting stuff happens. It's usually the most productive and diverse part of the whole system.

12. Creatively Use and Respond to Change

Change is inevitable. By making careful observations and then stepping in at the right time, we can make a positive outcome based on changes instead of negative ones.

THE BENEFITS OF PERMACULTURE

Permaculture has a bunch of benefits that make it an attractive choice for anyone who has land and is looking to grow food, from farmers all the way down to backyard gardeners. Some of the benefits include:

1. Reduced water usage
You can save on water bills by making use of wastewater and rainwater. Even for homeowners this is worthwhile, but for larger farms it really becomes a more cost effective and efficient way of watering your crops.

2. It costs less
Permaculture is more cost-effective than growing plants conventionally. You don't have to spend money on things like pesticides or fertilizers.

Since permaculture systems require less maintenance, usually all you need to do is water crops and occasionally mulch, they also save money in terms of labor.

3. Reduced waste
If you're using a permaculture system, nothing goes to waste. Garden waste, leaves, table scraps, and other waste products get turned into fertilizer or food for livestock.

Some permaculture enthusiasts take this further and even

make use of things like compost toilets to truly live a zero waste lifestyle. Making use of byproducts is what really makes permaculture sustainable.

4. Nature does most of the work

Once everything is correctly set up in your permaculture garden, it will take care of itself much more than a conventional one. (For more information on selecting the best plants for your garden, check out our article on permaculture plants.)

Water can be stored in human-made water features to attract birds, frogs, and other beneficial wildlife that will help remove pests as well. Companion planting similarly helps to keep insect problems to a minimum.

Permaculture gardens require a lot less maintenance overall.

5. Less pollution

Permaculture is a more natural way of growing food and the use of any motorized farm equipment like tractors is rare.

6. Less toxins

Permaculture uses natural fertilizers and pest control methods and is usually considered organic, so you're not getting exposed to all of the chemicals you might be if you're using pesticides and other artificial products on your crops.

7. Improved values

By practicing permaculture, you'll naturally develop more ethical and positive values like wasting less, only using as much as you need, reducing pollution, and helping others.

You'll promote green living through use of only natural fertilizers and pesticides.

8. More self-sufficiency

Permaculture allows a farmer or gardener to have a wider array of crops on their land. It gives you the self-reliance of being able to grow whatever you want or need to eat.

If there's extras leftover, you can always learn how to preserve it for later use.

9. Applicable to existing systems

Existing agricultural systems and land can be transitioned over to the principles of permaculture. Anywhere that you can typically grow food can be used for permaculture on a large or small scale.

COMMON PERMACULTURE PRACTICES

In the decades since Holmgren first wrote about permaculture, a wide variety of new techniques and practices that fall under the general umbrella of permaculture have sprung up and become included under the topic.

Here are some of the more common subcategories of permaculture.

1) Agroforestry

Agroforestry is an approach to permaculture that combines trees or shrubs along with livestock or crops. The name comes from the combination of agriculture and forestry.

These two seemingly separate fields work together to create more sustainable, healthy, profitable, and productive systems.

Under the heading of agroforestry, you have forest farming, which is really an entire permaculture topic unto itself. But the basic idea is to use a seven-layered system to create your food forest.

This includes a canopy layer, low tree layer, shrub layer,

herbaceous layer, rhizosphere, ground cover layer, and vertical layer.

It's designed to mimic naturally-occurring forests, but using nut and fruit trees, vegetables, herbs, and other plants that are useful for humans.

Other agroforestry systems include silvopastoral and silvoarable. Silvopastoral systems combine trees with foraging livestock, while silvoarable combines trees with companion crops.

Alley cropping is another agroforestry technique that involves cultivating food, specialty crops, or forage in between wide rows of trees.

As you might imagine, there is a lot of overlap between these different types of agroforestry and they have a lot in common, so the lines aren't always perfectly clear.

For example, alley cropping can be used as part of a silvoarable system.

What all types of agroforestry have in common is that they can help to improve crop production, diversify farm income, and provide protection and other benefits to crops.

Having nut trees alongside foraging livestock means that you get the benefits of additional income from the nuts that you gather.

The trees provide protection from the wind, rain and other elements for livestock and reduce the risk of mortality. And animals produce waste as they forge which in turn fertilizes the trees and boosts their production capacity.

• Examples of cultures around the world combining agriculture with forestry are surprisingly common. They stretch back hundreds of years or more, from Southeast Asia to North America.

2) Hügelkultur

Hügelkultur is German meaning "hill culture." It's a technique whereby large amounts of wood are buried to improve the water retention abilities of the soil.

This decaying wood acts like a sponge to hold onto water that seeps into the ground. Often compostable plant materials are planted on top of the mound and eventually composted into the soil as well.

A Hügelkultur is a great way to follow the permaculture principle of catching and storing energy.

Water during rainy times of year gets trapped in the underground wood, which can often hold enough volume to help keep plants alive even through an extended dry season.

This practice is a great alternative to burning wooden debris and other unwanted wood. Instead of releasing carbon into the atmosphere when it's burned, the wood's carbon gets sequestered back into the ground.

A Hügelkultur mound usually has a lifespan of 5 or 6 years before the wood fully rots and the process needs to be repeated again.

3) Harvesting Rainwater and Greywater

Instead of just letting rainwater run off your land, you can accumulate and store it to use later on. This is embodying the permaculture principle of "catch and store energy."

Most rainwater is collected from roofs. Homes, barns, and other structures on your farm likely already have eavestroughs that collect and move water away from the buildings.

To harvest rainwater, all you need to do is hook up a large tank to your downspout collect this water, instead of simply letting it soak into the ground and go to waste.

Another water catchment method is stormwater harvesting. It differs from rainwater harvesting in that it deals with the collection of stormwater from creeks, drains, and other waterways instead of from roofs.

One way farmers can create a stormwater harvesting system is by making a cistern or water reservoir at the base of a hill. This will catch most of the water which flows down the hillside.

The advantage to stormwater harvesting over rainwater harvesting is that a much larger volume of water than rainwater harvesting can. The downside is that it collects a larger amount of pollutants.

To mitigate this, normally rocks and silt are incorporated into the hill to partially filter the water before it arrives at the cistern.

Both rainwater and stormwater can be used for a variety of applications, including water for irrigation and livestock, as well as even drinking water if properly treated first.

What the water will be used for determines the extent to which it needs to be treated. The water would need to be screened, disinfected, and filtered before its potable for humans.

One final source of reusable water on the farm is greywater. This is water that comes from activities in the home or around the farm like taking a bath, washing dishes, or doing the laundry.

This water is different and kept separate from the black-water of toilets or septic systems, which is difficult to reuse.

Greywater can't be reused for drinking water since it contains soaps and detergents, but can be used for landscape irrigation and other purposes.

Human waste can be repurposed, although the process is harder and less practical. The two most common approaches are composting or using the material to create biogas.

Biogas is methane from human waste which can be used as a fuel for cooking or heating.

Even after composting, it's not recommended to use human manure on crops because of the high risk of pathogens and bacterial contamination, although they can be used on trees and shrubs.

Getting composting toilets approved by your local sanitation authorities can be a difficult ordeal, so they're less commonly used.

4) Cell Grazing

Grazing is usually seen as a negative activity that has the ability to destroy the environment if not practiced responsibly. And it's true that allowing livestock to overgraze an area can have negative consequences.

Under permaculture, cell grazing (also called rotational grazing) is the preferred method. This involves moving groups of livestock regularly between different fields, pastures, or forests.

Either ruminant animals (like cows, goats, and sheep) or non-ruminant animals (like pigs, rabbits, or flocks of geese) can be used effectively for cell grazing.

When done responsibly, the disturbances caused by grazing animals can actually prompt a better ecology and allow plants to regrow more quickly.

Cell grazing involves closely monitoring and monitoring livestock and how they're interacting with the land.

Plants need adequate rest between grazings, so it's important that an area gets a rest period to regrow after it has been grazed.

However, you also don't want to over rest an area or plants can go through lignification (become woody), resulting in lower productivity. So it's a delicate balancing act.

Even vegans and others opposed to using animals for meat, milk, or fiber can still keep livestock for grazing by using what's called conservation grazing.

This is the practice of using animals like sheep and goats to eat invasive plants, or allowing them to replace your lawnmower to keep grass short. Animal welfare is maximized, as they're closely monitored.

Farmers can ensure their livestock are getting sufficient quality and quantity of water, and their nutrition can be managed and supplementation provided as needed.

Conservation farming provides a low-stress environment for domestic animals while also allowing them to contribute productively to the farm and earn their keep.

5) Sheet Mulching

Many farmers and gardeners already make use of mulching, which is just any kind of protective cover placed on top of the soil to retain water and prevent weed growth.

Wood chips, cardboard, plastic, stones, and other materials are all commonly used.

Sheet mulching is an organic no-dig technique that tries to mimic the soil buildup that happens naturally in forests, namely how leaves cover the ground.

The practice of sheet mulching is also sometimes referred to as "lasagna gardening" since it uses many alternating layers of materials. In a cross-section, land that has had sheet mulching applied to it would look like a slice of lasagna.

Most commonly, sheet mulching uses alternating layers of "green" and "brown" materials. Brown materials include fallen leaves, shredded paper and cardboard, pine needles, wood chips, and straw.

Green materials include manure, grass clippings, worm casings, vegetable scraps, hay, coffee grounds, and compost.

Anywhere from 5 to 10 layers of materials may be used. Your sheet mulching should always be topped with straw or wood chips.

Sheet mulching helps add nutrients and organic matter to the soil, suppress weed growth, moderate temperatures and protect against frost, reduce erosion and evaporation, and absorbs rainfall.

6) Natural Building

Natural building is a more sustainable approach to construction than going down to your local hardware store or lumber yard for materials.

In a permaculture system, you should strive to use as many recycled or salvaged materials as is practical.

There are plenty of renewable resources on the land that you might be able to make use of in your next building project.

Clay, rocks, wood, reeds, straw, and sand are all readily available materials that most people overlook.

For example, subsoil, water, straw, and lime can be combined to create cob. This building material is very low cost, but it's also fireproof, resistant to seismic activities, and is strong enough to build entire houses out of.

Despite being made of natural materials, cob is very resistant to weathering. With proper maintenance, a cob structure will last a very long time.

In fact, the oldest cob house still standing is estimated to be 10,000 years old. Not bad, considering the cost to build a small cob house is only about $5,000 to $10,000.

Cob also allows for some very unique architecture that isn't possible with bricks or other traditional building materials, since you can mold it like clay into any shape that you want.

Adobe is another material similar to cob which is used all over the world, from Mexico to the Middle East.

Less natural materials like tires can also be used for construction. Earthship homes are a type of passive solar earth shelter that are constructed by stacking tires filled with earth to form walls, and then covering them.

This can be a great way to repurpose used tires that would otherwise end up in landfills or incinerated. Discarded glass windows are also often similarly used instead of buying new.

7) No-Till or Minimum-Till Farming

Minimum-till or no-till farming aims to leave soil undisturbed. Instead of breaking up the soil before planting, it's simply left undisturbed.

This helps retain water, prevents carbon from leaving the soil, improves soil quality, and reduces the amount of weed seeds being brought closer to the surface to germinate.

Conventional farming disturbs the soil. This lets carbon dioxide into the atmosphere and overly oxygenizes the soil.

Loosening the soil like this can also lead to erosion and nutrient runoff, as well as destroying beneficial fungi networks in the land.

With the proper techniques, tilling is something that can be minimized, or potentially even eliminated entirely for some systems.

8) Intercropping and Companion Planting

Intercropping is the combining of two or more plant species into an area which have beneficial effects on one another.

One example is companion planting, where strong-smelling plants and herbs like basil, oregano, chives, or garlic alongside main crops like tomatoes, carrots, or cabbage.

Pests hate the smell of many of these strong-smelling companion plants. Not only that, but some of them actually improve the growth and flavor of the plants they're paired with as well.

Others loosen the soil or give other benefits.

You will need to look up different plant companions and carefully plan your garden accordingly.

While many plants work well if combined with other plants, there are other plants that don't get along because they require the same nutrients, or for other reasons.

For example, carrots don't like to be planted near dill, sage attracts pests that feed on cucumbers, and most plants dislike being planted near fennel.

9) Market Gardening

Market gardening is an interesting move away from traditional agriculture, which is done on large tracts of land far out in the country, to smaller plots of land that are sometimes even located in urban environments.

Like the name suggests, market gardeners often sell their

produce at farmer's markets, although some may supply restaurants and grocery stores directly as well.

In market gardening, cash crops are intensively grown on a small scale (usually less than an acre of land.)

A market gardener can earn as much as $100,000 per year while growing on as little as a quarter acre of land. Permaculture and other sustainable practices are a big part of what makes this possible.

THE IMPORTANCE OF PERMACULTURE FARM DESIGN

Permaculture is crucial, because right now, it's the only food production system we have that's beyond sustainable.

Conventional agriculture tends not to be sustainable at all, so it's not really something to measure against. Really we should set the bar at sustainability because that's what's necessary for humanity to survive in the long term.

But really we strive for food production systems that will give a net positive result. Otherwise, the human population won't be able to grow and still have all of its food needs met.

So the goal of permaculture is to design a system where more energy gets extracted from the system over its lifetime than what you have to put in.

Usually, this involves working with a closed-loop system that incorporates waste products back into the system.

Permaculture is adaptable. It's constantly under development and permaculture farmers are constantly trying to find better and more efficient ways of doing things, and to have a better understanding of nature.

Biodiversity thrives under permaculture. We don't have to make the tradeoff of destroying forests and other habitats for wild plants and animals, just to produce our food or earn an income.

It's a way of people living more symbiotically and sustainably, and being better stewards of the environment while still getting our own needs met.

THE HISTORY OF PERMACULTURE

Permaculture as we know it today was originally developed by David Holmgren and Bill Mollinson of Australia in the 1970s.

It came about a decade after the world began to learn about the dangers of pesticides like DDT and the threat they posed to humans and the environment.

The term was made from a combination of the words "permanent" and "agriculture" since it was designed for the creation of sustainable (in other words, permanent) systems.

It was one of the first agricultural systems devised where we began to understand that local actions could have global impacts.

Although Holmgren is credited with popularizing permaculture, it's worth noting that several works on topics like agroforestry and forest farming had existed since the 1930s or earlier, and unwritten records of similar techniques most likely date back much farther than that.

FREQUENTLY ASKED QUESTIONS

Q: What is the difference between permaculture and organic farming?
A: Organic farming means not using chemical fertilizers, pesticides, or genetically modified organisms.

Permaculture includes organic farming practices, but goes beyond that and lays out larger systems about how a farm should be structured, how to reduce waste, and other important considerations as well.

Q: What is the difference between horticulture and permaculture?
A: Horticulture simply refers to the growing of plants for commercial consumption, usually vegetables. There is some overlap, and parts of permaculture can be classified as horticulture.

But horticulture also applies to other farming techniques like monoculture, and permaculture includes things like raising livestock that aren't part of horticulture.

Q: Where can I find permaculture farms near me?
A: Many permaculture farms are eager to show the great work they're doing to the public and allow visitors. But

there isn't necessarily one directory where you can look to find permaculture farms in your area.

I recommend doing a Google search for "permaculture farm + (your city)" to find farms in your area. Many of them will have websites or social media pages where you can contact them to learn more.

HOW TO START A PERMACULTURE GARDEN: STEP BY STEP BEGINNER'S GUIDE

If you're just starting your first garden, now is the perfect time to get started with permaculture while you're in the design phase. But even if you've already got an established garden, this guide will help you to slowly transition your existing garden to more sustainable design.

How do you start a permaculture garden? Decide where you will want your garden to go, observe your land and see what makes sense for your area, design your garden, add in water systems and other infrastructure, and then plant your perennials before annuals.

In this article, you'll learn what a permaculture garden is, how to make one step-by-step, the main permaculture principles to abide by, and some suggestions for real permaculture projects you can add to your own garden!

WHAT IS A PERMACULTURE GARDEN?

A permaculture garden is one that takes advantage of the aspects of nature like the sun, wind, and water, to work for you instead of against you.

Conventional gardening tends to have a one-size-fits-all approach. Take square foot gardening, for example. Although it's productive, it's not very natural.

Soil is made perfectly uniform and divided up into exact segments, with specific numbers of plants in each segment.

In contrast, a permaculture garden is more like art than science.

How you design your garden will depend on what makes the most sense for your particular piece of land, and the climate and ecosystems that already exist there.

Permaculture puts more emphasis on building up soils gradually over time so they're well balanced and full of nutrients.

Before you can start creating your own permaculture garden, first you have to understand what a permaculture garden really means to you.

Permaculture offers a lot of flexibility, and ultimately it's up to you to decide how you want to design and structure your garden.

You'll need to think about what your priorities are. Taking into account various factors like productivity, sustainability, aesthetics, and more.

You don't need a big backyard to get started with permaculture gardening. A small yard or even a balcony can be made into a productive garden.

Every little bit that we can do to live more sustainably makes a difference to the environment.

Whether you grow enough food to feed your family, or just enough tomatoes or fresh herbs that you need during the warmer months.

Or even just to have a bit of greenery to help you stay connected with nature and maybe help out local pollinating insects a little bit.

We can all use permaculture gardens to do our part.

A major component of creating a permaculture garden is design. Here are the 12 principles of permaculture that you'll want to incorporate into any garden that you create:

• Observe and Interact

• Catch and Store Energy

• Obtain a yield

• Apply Self-Regulation and Accept Feedback

- Use and Value Renewable Resources and Services

- Produce No Waste

- Design From Patterns to Details

- Integrate Rather Than Segregate

- Use Small and Slow Solutions

- Use and Value Diversity

- Use Edges and Value the Marginal

- Creatively Use and Respond to Change

In addition to these principles, you'll also want to take the 3 ethical tenants into account:

- Care for the earth

- Care for people

- Only take your fair share (and return any or share any surplus or waste)

These basic ideas will serve you well as you develop every part of your garden. From how you plan your garden design, to how you preserve resources like water and electricity.

Now that you have the basic mindset needed, let's talk about exactly how to go about starting your permaculture garden, step by step.

HOW TO START YOUR PERMACULTURE GARDEN

When you're first getting acquainted with permaculture, there's enough information out there to easily become overwhelmed.

It's hard to figure out for yourself what your priorities should be, and what needs to be done in which order. That's why I've created this handy step-by-step list to help you through every step of the way.

Feel free to refer back to this guide at any point along your journey if you're feeling lost.

Step 1 – Decide Where Your Garden Will Go
If you already have a fairly large backyard, that's the most obvious place to get started with your garden. The only factor you'll need to consider is in which part of the yard your garden will go.

For other people without such easy access to land, they might already get hung up at this step before they even begin.

Don't fret if you're thinking to yourself, "But I live in an apartment!"

There are ways to help start your own permaculture garden or help contribute to other people's gardens regardless of whether you have access to land of your own or not.

If you haven't even got a balcony, then I'd highly recommend joining a community garden. Most cities nowadays have plots of public land set aside where people can collectively garden.

I'd highly recommend it, as it's a great opportunity to meet other gardeners who likely have years of experience and advice to share.

You'll want to sign up for an allotment right away if you're interested though, as the waiting list in some places can be long. If no spaces are currently free, you might have to wait until one is available to claim.

If you rent an apartment, you can ask your landlord if it would be possible to create a garden on the roof. This would have been unheard of years ago.

But now many cities around the world are offering tax credits to building owners who add green roofs to their structures.

So the building owner might be happy to let you grow plants on the roof in exchange for being able to take advantage of such a tax savings.

If you have nearby friends who have a yard, ask if they'd be willing to let you use a portion of their yard to create a permaculture garden.

Many homeowners would be happy to let you do this in exchange for a portion of the produce you harvest, or an agreement to weed and tend to the existing flowerbeds in their yard as well.

Permaculture gardening can be done in almost any shape and size. So don't get too hung up on not having the perfect piece of land. It's more about the ideas and principles than how much food you end up growing.

So don't give up. Where there's a will, there's a way!

Step 2 – Observe Your Land

Before you make any decisions about how you're going to plan out your garden, it's best to just take a moment and observe what already exists on the land that you're planning to use.

This step might seem obvious, but don't skip it.

After looking out at your yard hundreds of times, you may feel like you know everything about it. But if you actually get out and take a walk around to immerse yourself in it, you may find out things you didn't know.

1. Is there actually a bit of a slope in one section of your yard?

2. Does the ground seem to pool in one part of the yard after it rains, where it might be too wet for things to grow?

3. Do you have a big tree in your yard where you won't want to plant, because the ground is too full of roots and its leaves will block out too much sunlight?

4. What kinds of animals and insects (both beneficial and pests) do you see as you look around?

5. Do you have any unique resources or features you can take advantage of?

6. What areas get the most sun in the morning versus the afternoon?

These are just a few of the questions you should ask yourself.

STEP 3 – DESIGN YOUR GARDEN

Design Your Garden

Design and planning is a huge part of permaculture, so don't skimp on this step either. A good design will save you lots of effort, while a poorly designed garden will be a thorn in your side for many years to come.

Based on your initial observations, you should have a good idea of different factors such as shade, elevation, and areas where children will play or people will gather which you can plan around.

Also take note of water sources you'll use and plan around them. Whether that's a water tap on the outside of your home, a pond, or something else.

From personal experience, I can tell you that placing your garden 50 feet from a water source and up a hill isn't the wisest choice, and you'll probably come to regret it!

Think about where you want to put various annual or perennial plants, and how much space they'll take up as they grow over time.

I recommend trying to make a detailed sketch of your garden plans, rather than just having a vague idea in your head and trying to wing it.

When you put it down on paper, you might realize some aspect of it doesn't make sense. And it's a lot easier to take out your eraser and fix it at that point, instead of doing it once you're out working in the dirt.

You can always change your design as your goals or needs change. Taking a few minutes to measure out your yard will allow you to make a more accurate drawing.

Or if you're struggling, you can use the satellite view from Google Maps to get a basic shape.

STEP 4 – PUT IN WATER SYSTEMS AND OTHER INFRASTRUCTURE

Water systems can be the difference between your permaculture garden succeeding or failing. Water is a valuable resource that you need to keep and use in sustainable ways.

During the design phase you should have figured out which areas of your property water tends to pool, where it runs away from your property, and where water is needed the most.

Depending on how much space you have to work with, you might want to put in a swale (a ditch where water can collect) where water is naturally pooling anyway.

Or you can set up rain capture from your roof to be stored in barrels or cisterns, so you can use it for watering or washing crops and tools.

STEP 5 – BUILD AND PREPARE YOUR BEDS

Permaculture generally calls for doing the least destructive changes possible, so once you decide where your garden is going to go, your best bet is probably sheet mulching or spot planting.

Sheet mulching, also called lasagna gardening, is a way of creating a larger plantable area.

It's called lasagna gardening because it involves stacking alternating layers of materials like leaves, straw, wood chips, cardboard, compost, and others in a way that would look like a slice of lasagna as a cross-section.

Grass doesn't need to be dug up, you simply start mulching on top of it, and the grass underneath will die and become part of the soil as well.

Sheet mulching takes less effort than having to remove grass and till the soil before planting.

Plus it doesn't disturb microbes in the soil, or stir up weed seeds that may be buried underground and cause them to germinate.

Sheet mulching takes time before the materials will decompose though, so it's best to mulch in the fall so that you can begin planting in that area in the spring.

Spot planting is useful for covering smaller areas. You can dig a hole or remove a small section of grass and then plant into the soil. The benefit of spot planting is that plants can start growing right away with this method.

So if you want to start a garden and it's already spring or summer, this might be a better option for you.

The downside is that you don't get nutrients added to the soil like with sheet mulching, so you may need to amend the soil with compost or an organic slow-release fertilizer.

It's also a good idea to cover the area with straw as a mulch when you're done planting, to help suppress weeds and keep in water.

STEP 6 – PLANT PERENNIALS FIRST

The first stage of planting your garden should be worrying about where the perennials will go. Because these are the plants that are going to come up year after year, and they'll be a regular staple of the garden.

You'll want to be sure to pick crops that make sense for your planting zone. Trying to grow lemons in Minnesota or the UK makes a lot less sense than in Florida or Spain.

If possible, pick native plants, as they'll be the best suited for your area of all. You should be able to find plants that meet those criteria but still provide the fuel, fiber, and food that you need.

You can plant perennials from seed, but many of them like asparagus or fruit trees will take several years before they start to produce, so it's better to get some transplants or bare-root saplings to minimize the time before you're able to start harvesting from them.

Check local garden clubs in your area to find less-common plants, or worst-case many nurseries have the option to order online or by mail order.

But buying from a local nursery is always your best choice, since the plants will already be adapted for your climate, weather conditions, and soil.

If you've got friends who are also looking to start a garden, you can buy as a group to take advantage of lower bulk prices.

Once you've got ahold of the perennials that you want, you can stop planning and actually start to get your hands dirty! If you have the budget for it, it's good to plant a bit closer together than recommended.

That way you can choose the healthiest plants later on and remove the rest to be used for compost. Planting more densely initially will help stop the growth of weeds as well.

At this point you can also start some companion planting. Like placing onions and chives under trees to prevent digging pests and disease. Or flowers to help begin attracting pollinators.

STEP 7 – ADD IN ANNUALS

Your permaculture garden probably isn't going to look like much of a garden yet, after all you've added in so far is perennials.

You might have a bunch of young fruit and nut trees, and some asparagus and rhubarb and other transplants. But overall your garden probably just looks like a bunch of twigs at this point.

For the first few years of your garden, you probably want to add in lots of annuals to fill all the extra space, while your perennials are still taking root.

The good news is that most of the popular and well-known vegetables we enjoy are annuals. Like beans, peas, tomatoes, peppers, squash, and others.

You can also add in flowers and lots of greens to give more of a permaculture look to your garden.

Sunflowers are a great plant for filling lots of space.

Plus they're low maintenance, you'll get lots of seeds from them if you're lucky, and you can chop and drop their large stalks at the end of the growing season to add a bunch of nutrients back into the soil.

If you're relying on your garden for either food or income,

annuals will definitely make up the bulk of either for your first couple of years.

STEP 8 – WATCH YOUR GARDEN GROW AND MAINTAIN IT

Starting a permaculture garden can seem like an overwhelming amount of work at first.

But once you've got all your plants in the ground and you're into a routine of watering and tending to everything, don't forget to take a step back and appreciate what you've got.

Your garden should give you joy just to observe and be around if you're passionate about it. Take this opportunity to learn how your garden works.

Watch all of the wildlife that comes and goes, and see how various plant species grow and bloom for the first time.

You'll get to enjoy the harvest of your healthiest and fastest-producing plants in your first year, but a lot of the initial reward will just be seeing what's successful and working in general.

Set some time aside every week or so to do some weeding. If you deal with weeds regularly, it's not too bad. But if you leave them for too long, they can quickly get out of control.

STEP 9 –
COMPOSTING

As your first season starts to draw to a close, you'll likely have a bunch of leftover plant matter. Now is the perfect time to really get your composting going, so you'll have some extra nutrient-rich soil ready for next year.
Remember the principles of permaculture and try to run your garden as waste-free as possible, reincorporating any waste products back into the system.

There are lots of different composter designs to choose from. You can get a continuous composter, which is the black single-body composter that you're probably familiar with.

Just add your yard waste and kitchen scraps to it over time, and there's very little maintenance required.

Or you can use a batch or tumbling composter to accelerate the decomposition, but you'll need to rotate it daily and make sure it has enough moisture.

It's also possible to use indoor composters or worm bins, although I wouldn't recommend these for gardeners, as you'll likely have a lot more organic material than what these are meant to handle.

Step 10 – Get Involved With Your Community

There are lots of other gardeners out there who are just as passionate about permaculture as you are. Find a local group and get involved.

Whether you meet other beginner gardeners who you can share the journey with, or advanced gardeners who can mentor you and answer any questions you have, everyone benefits from joining together and sharing information about their gardens, what's working and what's not, and the latest trends they're keeping up on.

You can also volunteer to help with community gardens, donate some vegetables from your permaculture garden to a local food bank, or find other ways to use your passion for sustainable agriculture to give back.

A FINAL NOTE –
JUST GET STARTED!

Chances are that you've read the above steps, but you haven't even started with the first step yet. So I'd just encourage you to get started.

Just getting started can be a big hurdle to get over, and it's easy to feel overwhelmed, or experience analysis paralysis and get stuck on every small detail.

The truth is that your permaculture garden is never going to be perfect during your first season. You just have to get started, and some of your most valuable lessons will come from the direct experience of trying for yourself.

There are some things that you just can't pick up from books or Youtube videos.

A great way to get started is to break your big project down into smaller parts, and take care of them one little piece at a time.

Starting small will also help you from being overambitious and biting off more than you can chew, which more often than not will burn you out and make you want to give up.

PERMACULTURE GARDEN PRACTICES

Still not sure how to get started on your permaculture garden? Here are some real techniques and designs to give you some inspiration and get you started.

1. No-Dig Gardening

No-dig gardening is a common permaculture idea that helps protect the soil microbiome that helps to transform organic matter into our food.

Sheet mulching is one example of no-dig gardening that we touched on earlier. Other popular no dig methods include raised beds and hugelkultur.

Permaculture gardeners want to avoid digging because it can kill beneficial bacteria, organisms, and creatures that keep the soil healthy.

So no-dig garden beds are made on top of existing soil, or even grass, without disturbing it. Adding mulch helps to retain water and cut down on weeds.

2. Worm Composting

Another option besides conventional composting is to make use of worm composting.

Put your plant debris and kitchen scraps into large buckets

or bins which have composting worms in them. Regular earthworms will work nicely.

The worms will eat these scraps and turn them into worm castings, which have more nutrients for the soil than just ordinary compost would.

You can buy some worms from a bait shop, or better yet, just capture your own from your garden. After you've got some, just drill a bunch of coin-sized holes in the bottom of a large 5 gallon bucket. Then bury it halfway into your garden and fill it with shredded cardboard and paper, and add a layer of soil or dried grass on to the top.

As the worm castings are created, they'll drain directly out the holes in the bottom of the bucket and provide nutrients to the surrounding soil. But even with holes in the bucket, it will still fill with worm castings over time.

At that point, you can empty your bucket over your garden bed and repeat the process.

3. Keyhole Gardens

Keyhole gardens are one example where taking other gardening methods from around the world can lead to improvements over conventional gardening.

A keyhole garden is a raised bed with an indentation or chunk in one side of it. This allows gardeners to get in closer to the garden, where they can weed, maintain, water, and harvest easily from all areas of the bed.

Less bending over and stretching is needed compared to a regular garden, which is great for the elderly or anyone with mobility issues.

In addition to their layout, keyhole gardens also encourage mixing plants together to encourage biodiversity, instead of just growing rows of single crops. That way they're less at risk of developing diseases or pests.

Keyhole gardens allow all of the cultivated land to be utilized, as opposed to conventional gardening where we might create garden beds where portions are too far to effectively reach and use.

4. Chop and Drop

If the thought of taking all of your garden scraps to the composter seems like too much work, you don't have to feel guilty about it. Chop and drop is a technique that can help!

Chop and drop is where you simply remove plant material from your garden at the end of the season, cut it into pieces, and drop it right onto the soil where it was growing.

This technique can help add nitrogen to the soil, and act as an organic mulch that prevents evaporation and moderates soil temperature. It also stops the wind and rain from eroding topsoil.

With the chop and drop method, your whole garden can act as a composter, and you can simply let materials decompose where they were originally growing.

You can also go a step further and create what's called green manure. This is where soil amending crops are grown specifically so they can be turned into the soil to add nutrients.

5. Companion Gardening

Many plants have synergistic effects on each other. Some plants provide nutrients that other plants need to thrive, others improve the yield or flavor of certain vegetables, while others keep pests away.

Biodiversity is how nature meant for plants to grow, so don't feel like you need to conform to the norm of planting a single type of crop in a row.

Corns, beans, and squash are one of the most popular combinations of complementary plants. Corn grows up into the air, beans can climb up the corn stalks as natural poles, and squash spreads out along the ground.

All three of these plants also have positive relationships underground at the root level as well, to boost the growth and production of all three.

CONCLUSION

Permaculture is a great way to continue generating high yields and maintain your current level of productivity, even if you're switching away from a more conventional farming model or system.

It gives a more environmentally-friendly and sustainable system for agriculture by taking a more holistic approach to managing livestock and crops.

Not only can permaculture be just as profitable as conventional farming, it's often easier and less labor-intensive as well.

This is because using the 12 principles of permaculture, you allow nature to work for you, instead of trying to work against it.